This Emerging Wisdom

Copyright © 2024 by Sharron Montague Loree

All rights reserved
No portion of this book may be reproduced, stored in a retrieval system, or transmitted in any form by any means—electronic, mechanical, photocopy, recording, or other—except for brief quotations in printed reviews, without prior permission of the author.

Paperback ISBN: 9798822960428

This Emerging Wisdom

Sharron Montague Loree

DEDICATION

This book positively could not have been done alone. I'm indebted to seven people for their unique contributions.

To Jared Emery, editor extraordinaire, for tirelessly evaluating multicultural proverbs for months.

To Joshua Olusoji-lordreigns for having the great idea that made this book possible and for his amazingly, beautiful cover art, thank you so much.

To my son, Julian Loree Cash, for locating many fascinating, esoteric proverbs.

To my daughter, Megan Montague Cash, for helping me design the covers.

To my cousin, Shelly Munoz, for self-publishing several of my books.

To Valerie Paradiz, for continuous advice and encouragement and for writing superb book reviews for me.

Finally, for my wise granddaughter, Winter Cash, whose sayings appear in this book, my many thanks again.

FOREWORD

This Emerging Wisdom offers a rich buffet of truisms, pithy humor, sage advice and brilliant gems of human insight. Keep it by your bedside. Use it in a daily routine of prayer, meditation or those sometimes hard to grasp restorative moments of solitude. Sharron Montague Loree has crafted this lovely book to be your loyal companion.

Valerie Paradiz
author of Elijah's Cup, a book about autism
and Clever Maids, a book about Grimm's Fairy Tales

PREFACE

Only my curiosity and patience has qualified me to put together a book about wisdom. I am not particularly wise. I'm just a Hippie artist who loves to research interesting topics.

When I became curious about multicultural wisdom, I researched using my notebooks, my books, my friend's books and the internet.

Wisdom is not stuffy, it is down-to-earth, basic, and essential.

I have fallen in love with an artform called, "proverbs". A proverb is a short saying which gives a piece of advice. Proverbs are often elegant and funny.

I have included many proverbs from all around the world in this second edition of This Emerging Wisdom.

INTRODUCTION

There are 195 countries in the world. Every country has its own proverbs. You can tell a lot about a country by its proverbs.

Some countries feature proverbs about one person's achievement and individual success. Some other countries care more about communal unity and everyone getting along well together.

Some small countries have only a dozen proverbs and some other countries have over a thousand.

Proverbs are a very important aspect of some cultures. The Yoruba culture in Nigeria loves proverbs, so they have thousands of them.

Some proverbs may be thousands of years old. There

is no way to ever know which person said a proverb. Many sayings were coined centuries ago, but they still remain relevant today. All proverbs are in the public domain. A proverb is an old phrase with no author.

Proverbs, with their wisdom, have a unique position in the field of mental health. Reflecting on timeless truths can help us push our personal development forward. The truth can offer solace during difficult times. Knowing that one is trying to be a considerate person can improve one's self esteem. A person could become grounded in ethics and morality.

Wise people are good people who will look out for the best interests of everyone.

Wisdom improves awareness. It helps us evaluate situations correctly and make good choices. Wisdom opens the way.

THIS EMERGING WISDOM

1

If you have wisdom,
you will make choices that bring joy.

2

A book is like a garden
carried in the pocket.

3

Be happy if there is no reason to be sad.

4

Cultivate a heart of love
that knows no anger.

5

Persevere, like a bird in the wind.

6

The time eventually comes
when seeking is over and finding begins.

7

Truth may walk through the world, unarmed.

8

Appreciate people whose kindness
isn't a strategy,
but a way of life.

9

If you would live long, open your heart.

10

Care and not fine stables makes a good horse.

11

Be Someone's Miracle

12

Choose the power of love,
over the love of power.

13

The slow but humble turtle overtakes
the fast but arrogant rabbit.

14

Everyone smiles and laughs
in the same language.

15

Being extended an invitation to dine
does not make you a kinsman.

16

Even in your desire for wisdom,
steer a middle course.

17

Ten lands are sooner known,
than one person.

18

In 'The Kingdom Of Hope'
there is no winter.
Whether you are young or old,
live with hope.

19

We have been conditioned
to be too serious.
Finding the humor in things
is the best habit we can acquire.

20

Talking can get you in trouble.
Before speaking,
let your words pass through your heart.

21

What a person thinks, is who they are.

22

Judge not thy neighbor.
In their heart, they have secrets
that could make you weep.

23

Even as a solid rock
is unshaken by the wind,
so are the wise
unshaken by praise or blame.

24

One day is for you and another day is against you.
Every day is a fishing day,
but not every day is a catching day.

25

A person should stay alive, if only out of curiosity.
Never give up on life.

26

Red sky at night, sailor's delight.
Red sky in the morning, sailor's warning.

27

The one who is wrong,
constantly justifies themselves for everything.

28

One kind word
can warm three winter months.

29

If a little money does not go out,
great money will not come in.
One who doesn't risk a penny,
won't make a peso.

30

The lucky eagle
kills a mouse that has eaten salt.

31

The youths are wise.
The elders are wise.
Age is honorable and youth is noble.

32

A swift response is the sweetest.

33

Joy shared is twice the joy.
Sorrow shared is half the sorrow.

34

People are attracted to
the spiritual purity of inner goodness.

35

Learn from your mistakes,
It's a fantastic education.
This earth is a school.

36

Problems are to humble us, not to tumble us.

37

God, who is cooking the soup,
has not left the kitchen.

38

Don't look at the gift received,
but at the intention of the giver.
It's the thought that counts.

39

The one who loves does not hate.

40

Nothing is sillier
than taking everything too seriously.
Be casual.

41

You are responsible
for your own happiness.
May your life be full of happiness.

42

Money talks. Dog barks. Money is not life.

43

If someone pushes your buttons,
wear clothes that don't have any buttons.

44

Don't provoke a jaguar with a short stick.

45

Riches don't transform character,
they expose it.

46

You won't ever catch up to
something that doesn't exist,
even on a fast horse.

47

The tall one wouldn't bend
and the short one wouldn't stretch,
so their kiss was lost.

48

Integrity comes from being in sync
with what is morally correct.

49

If a donkey kicks you and you kick back,
you are both donkeys.

50

Reality is astonishing!!!

51

The person who says that
something is impossible,
should not interrupt the one
who is doing the impossible.

52

Tell the truth at all times,
even when it is inconvenient to.

53

If you see a wrong-doing and you say nothing
against it,
you may become its victim as well.

54

When God is cooking,
you don't smell smoke.

55

Be precise.
The beginning of wisdom
is calling things by their right names.

56

Visiting is good,
but home is better.

57

The sins we often regret
are the sins we didn't commit.

58

Keep your pride in your pocket.

59

Pearls are of no value in the desert.

60

Operate from the inside out,
rather than from the outside in.

61

Be brave enough to use your intellect.

62

An ill-mannered person
is like a horse without a bridle.
Good manners are part and parcel
of a good education.

63

Give a person a fish,
and you feed them for a day.
Give them a cell-phone
and they won't bother you for weeks.

64

"I have a lot to say", said the fish,
"but my mouth is full of water."

65

The house of the heart is never full.
Saying "Hi" to literally everybody is awesome.

66

To ignore the plight of another
is to deny the humanity within oneself.

67

If you want everything you see,
you could eventually lose it all.

68

If you are on a road to nowhere,
find another road.

69

Respect is due, even to a dog or a cat.
Everyone understands kindness.

70

A liar better have a good memory.
The truth rises to the surface,
like oil on water.
There is usually no secret
that will not become evident.

71

If you find yourself in a disturbing situation,
try to look at it as: 'a learning experience'.

72

You can avoid ever being disappointed,
if you have no desires or preferences.

73

Something on your mind troubles you
until you speak about it.

74

When you help someone,
you can test your power of sacrifice.

75

The excess of a virtue is a vice.

76

Between true friends,
even the water they drink together
is enough.

77

Find your own way.
There is wisdom already inside you.

78

Speak well of your friend,
of your enemy, say nothing.

79

If your right hand is angry,
hold it back with your left,
or you could sit on your hands,
to remain peaceful.

80

The sheep contemplates in silence,
but its cunning thoughts number 1,400.

81

One muddy buffalo
makes the whole herd dirty.

82

Take the old, familiar, long road
to arrive safely.
Even if you travel slowly,
you will reach your destination.

83

A clear conscience shines.

84

A hedge between,
keeps friendship green.

85

Get up!
God helps an early riser.
An early bird will hop farther.

86

Do the right thing.

87

Choose the light.

88

A golden key can open any door.

89

Love is the glue that holds a family together.

90

Illness and activism
are the rents we must sometimes pay,
to live on this earth.

91

People don't care how much you know,
until they know how much you care.

92

A person is not a harmonica
that you put aside after you have used it.

93

If you want to understand
the height of a mountain,
climb up to its top.

94

The light shines even in a mouse hole.

95

It is better to fall while sitting
than to fall while standing.

96

For the soul there is no death.
We are truly timeless.
Here's to Eternity

97

For children, playing is not a luxury,
it is a necessity.
Playing is children's best way of learning.

98

Dip your tongue in wisdom,
then give advice.

99

Common sense is better than velvet.

100

Instead of choosing, go with the flow.
Let everything happen naturally.

101

It's better to be guilty in the eyes of people,
than in the eyes of God.

102

Help people who feel worthless,
to know that they are worthy.

103

The fabric of society is strongest
when it's woven with diverse threads.

104

A basic rule of caution,
don't be overly cautious.

105

The best friends are the fewest.

106

If a family lives in harmony,
all their affairs will prosper.

107

Even a rabbit looks at the moon.

108

Learning is a weightless treasure
that you can carry easily.

109

Every joke has an element of truth in it.

110

If you are a captain,
don't forget what it was like to be a sailor.

111

Don't burn your bridges.
Someday you may need those people,
or they may need you.
A fool hath said,
"All the bridges I burnt, lit my way!"

112

An accident doesn't come
with a bell around its neck.
Distrust is a good attitude to have for safety.

113

You have to tolerate
the kicks of the cow who gives you milk.

114

We share the earth with the tree people,
the creepy crawlers, the two leggeds,
the four leggeds, the swimmers in the water
and the little people of the air.

115

Celebrate diversity of identities.
Variety makes life delightful
and much more interesting.

116

When you take one step toward God,
God will take seven steps toward you.

117

If you agree with people,
they will think you are wise,
but always be authentic.

118

All the people live under one sky.
When the sun rises, it rises for everyone.

119

Those in easy circumstances
cannot always understand
the hardships of others.

120

The poor lack a lot,
but the greedy lack more.
Sometimes abundance causes arrogance.

121

We notice the faults of others,
and easily forget our own.

122

Selfish people don't know
how to show regret or ask for forgiveness.
When they should apologize,
they are silent.

123

One who has no sense of shame
always does as they please.
One who has no shame
owns the whole world.

124

Our relatives do not guarantee
merciful support.
Help comes only from those
divinely sent to help us.

125

A leaky roof tricks the sun,
but it does not deceive the rain.

126

A wise person
could try to leave their wisdom
to their heirs.

127

You may not realize a person's worth
until they are gone.

128

If you don't want any disappointments,
don't indulge in illusions.

129

At the top of the mountain, all paths meet.
Ten people, ten colors:
Our differences can bring us together.

130

No one interacts with
our flower-bedecked
God and loses.

131

When you are traveling,
rising early makes the road short.

132

Few can say of their house;
"There is no trouble here."
There are misfortunes or tragedies
in every family.

133

There are no privileged places.
The center of the universe is everywhere.
Sometimes it's best to just stay put.
If you leave a place where you are loved,
you could end up at a place
where you are irrelevant.

134

When the rabbit leaps,
there are no lame greyhounds.

135

A tongue's slip is a truth's revelation.

136

If you find yourself in a hole,
the first thing to do is stop digging.

137

Everytime you find humor
in a difficult situation,
you win.

138

Contentment is a point of view.

139

Avoid the pleasures
that will bite tomorrow.
Habits are first cobwebs, then cables.

140

When money talks: everyone else is silent.
Money says: "I am not at home,
let no one deliberate in my absence."

141

It's the desire to give, that gives.

142

A good deed is the best form of prayer.
Sow good deeds.

143

A person who finds discontentment
in one place,
is not likely to find happiness in another.

144

Every fool is pleased with their own folly.

145

When you are young,
hardship is valuable.

146

To those who love us,
love us and to those who don't,
may God break their leg
so we will know them by their limping.

147

If you can walk you can dance.
If you can talk, you can sing.

148

Those who are lucky in love,
don't have to be lucky in anything else.

149

You must shift your sail with the wind.

150

Some will learn through pain and sorrow,
others will learn through joy and laughter.
It's the same life,
whether we spend it crying or laughing.

151

One who gets angry, grows old fast.

152

Worries go down better with soup.

153

The gentle strides of a tiger
do not indicate cowardice.

154

Don't use people to get things.
Use things to help people.

155

Have the spiritual courage
to live up to your principles.

156

Get to know a person
before you reject them.

157

All waiting is long. The secret of patience
is to do something fun in the meantime.

158

Do your best,
then, don't worry, be happy.

159

Worry gives a small thing, a big shadow.
Most of the things we worry about,
never happen.

160

If you have the courage
to recognize your major mistakes,
you are on the road to wisdom.

161

A rich person will always have friends.

162

When you shoot an arrow of truth,
dip its point in honey.

163

If you go to a donkey's house,
don't talk about ears.

164

Time is gold.
Time cannot wait.
When time goes, it goes completely.

165

Go where the people
are kind and authentic.
Try to avoid mean people and fake people.

166

A weapon is an enemy even for its owner.

167

Who loses a friend goes down one step.

168

The mind is free
and the slightest thought
has great influence.
It is important
that we think enlightened thoughts.

169

The highest form of wisdom is compassion.

170

A guilty conscience is a hidden enemy.
Feel sorry for your misdeeds.

171

One who follows the right path,
thorns will not hurt them,
but don't walk on a pile of thorns,
because you have faith in your karma.

172

It is natural for people
to behave in a loving way.

173

Water is an antidepressant.
Negative ions in water
have an impact on one's brain.
Even a bath or a shower
can make a difference.

174

Non-violence is the supreme law of life.

175

Old ravens are not easy to fool.

176

Never miss an opportunity
to make people happy,
even if you have to leave them alone
in order to do it.

177

Jolly companions make life tolerable.

178

When they came to milk the cow,
she said, "I am an ox".
When they came to harness her,
she said, "I am a cow".

179

Farmers plant and harvest,
God alone knows
how the yams are formed.

180

Fall seven times,
stand up eight.

181

A virtuous person sleeps well,
their good conscience makes a soft pillow.

182

If people are mean to you,
they reveal who they are, not who you are.

183

You have to walk to go far.
If you run, you could fall.

184

Earth is the queen of beds.

185

A camel driver has their plans,
a camel has theirs.

186

Be discreet about what you repeat.
A wise person covereth the matter.

187

A Paradise without people
is not worth stepping a foot in.

188

Simple, innocent people
from the mountains,
purify the air
and make the earth wholesome.

189

Don't judge people by their defects,
just notice their many virtues.
One who looks for a friend without faults
will have no friends.

190

Simplify your life.
Be a Hippie.

191

Say pretty things and hear pretty things.
Sweet talk is the perfume of the heart.

192

What is demanded of a genius
is patience and the love of the truth.

193

Listening to someone lie
is like drinking warm water or cold soup.
The soul doesn't like being lied to.

194

"Waltz faster!" said the rebel,
"they are playing a tango!"

195

Begin to weave
and God will provide the thread.

196

Humans are all wonderfully different,
and we are all equally unique.

197

The real journey of discovery
begins in old age.
You can still learn new, important things
and do old, important things differently.
Life is long.

198

A piece of bread in the pocket
is better than a feather in the hat.

199

If we don't fight we remain equals.
If we do fight,
then one of us becomes the loser.

200

Wit in speech is like salt in food.

201

Hike up to the highlands, to see the lowlands.
The world reveals itself well to those who travel on foot.

202

One who afflicts us,
gives us experience that makes us wiser.

203

Be careful of what you ask for,
because you might get it.

204

It's better for them to be together,
than to spoil things for two other people.

205

Don't look for bad things
in the good that you do.

206

Lower your voice during an argument.
Yelling during a disagreement
adds fuel to the fire.

207

If life hands you lemons,
cook ocean perch.

208

Each person has to live
according to their own lights.

209

To be awake
is to be aware
of the cries of the marginalized.

210

Even a hut feels like paradise
when you are with your loved one.

211

The wise person never says,
"I did not think".

212

Poverty does not destroy virtue,
nor does wealth bestow it.

213

There is no use waiting
for your ship to come in,
unless you have sent one out.

214

Patience is a golden path.

215

It's much easier to swim
in the direction of the current.
Go with the flow.

216

One cooked bird in your hand
is better than a thousand birds flying.

217

Spending money on experiences
is better than spending on possessions,
but you can experience a possession
many times.

218

A seabird on solid ground
can mean that a storm is coming.

219

Good leaders stay hidden.
The people turn to each other and they say:
"We did it ourselves."
Power To The People!

220

When the cat is not home
the mice have a party
and dance on the table.

221

Help your friend's boat across
and your own will reach the shore.

222

When love reigns,
the impossible may be attained.

223

On the way to one's beloved,
there are no hills.

224

If you can't live longer,
live deeper.

225

The opportunities that God sends
do not wake up every sleeping person.

226

A sage brings peace.
A sage may not get angry,
but if they do,
they will not stay angry for long,

227

Anyone without domestic trouble
should be in bliss.

228

Smiling will gain you
ten more years of life.

229

One who falls by themselves doesn't cry.

230

When you have a lot to do,
start with a meal.

231

A gentle, kind word can open an iron gate.

232

There is no bad weather,
there is just bad clothing.

233

People who stay in their comfort zones learn a lot less.

234

Water that has been begged for
does not quench thirst.

235

Don't tell your children
what to do too often,
help them learn who they are.

236

A good person
triumphs when they are fair.

237

Once a person cheats,
forever people will distrust them.

238

Don't complain about lack of wind,
learn to sail.

239

Don't throw yourself into a trouble
that is not yours.

240

Your conscience is your compass,
it is God's voice.

241

Don't buy a house
until after you have met the neighbors.

242

There must be a reason
for continuous rebuke.

243

The children of your children
are sweeter than honey.

244

"La vie est belle!" means:
"Life is beautiful!"

245

Dumplings are better
than cherry blossoms.

246

Fate had us meet
from hundreds of miles away.

247

Don't change to make someone love you.
Be yourself,
and let the right person
fall for the real you.

248

A bird that allows itself to be caught,
will find a way of escaping.

249

Excessive boasting is despicable.

250

A sage opens the way.

251

Don't deny a child the opportunity
to solve their own problems.

252

Don't kick the bowl
after you have eaten all of the porridge.

253

Some people are so poor
that all they have is money.
A heart free from care
is better than a full purse.

254

When a person is loved,
they know that they matter.

255

The first step in wisdom
is bowing down to God.
Only fools thumb their noses
at someone powerful enough
to make the sun, the moon,
galaxies and trees.

256

Don't let bad circumstances steal your joy.

257

Survival is the treasured goal.

258

Anger can be an expensive luxury.

259

Growing old, one's sight worsens,
but this allows one to see more clearly.
One's hearing worsens,
but this allows one to hear more clearly.

260

It is not what they profess,
but what they practice
that makes them good.

261

Smooth seas do not make skillful sailors.
Only storms make good captains.

262

The higher you climb, the heavier you fall.

263

If you try to please every person,
you will please some of them.

264

Love knows hidden paths.

265

Throw a resourceful person in a river,
and they will probably come up
with a fish in their hand.

266

A good reputation
is better than golden clothing.

267

Too many opinions sink the ship.

268

In times of test,
family is best.

269

If your glass is half empty,
use a smaller glass.

270

Only God knows
why the wings of some birds are shorter.

271

You must walk around a little,
before you can understand
the distance from the valley to the mountain.

272

A person with good manners
tries not to show their anger.

273

The road is open for the rich.

274

A new thing is exciting.

275

You can't straighten a dog's tail.

276

If you are tolerant in one moment of fury,
you can prevent a year of regret.

277

For great ills, we need great remedies.

278

A good laugh and a long sleep
are great cures.

279

If we must compete,
we could compete to see
which person can be the most loving.

280

Keep a green tree in your heart,
and perhaps a singing bird will come.

281

Life is so short,
we must move very slowly.

282

You cannot drive straight
on a twisting road.

283

Put your good where it will do the most,
then brace yourself,
because no good deed goes unpunished.

284

Unto all things and all beings,
we shall be as relatives.

285

If a capable person lights a fire,
it will flare up even at the bottom of the sea,
while if one incapable does it,
it won't flare up even on land.

286

Don't believe everything you hear
and don't tell everything you believe.

287

If you live in a mud hut,
beware of the rain.

288

Most people seem to be normal,
until you get to know them.

289

A heart that loves is always young.

290

Many little things
can make a person love someone
in a big way.

291

You can live a simple, ordinary life,
in an exceptional manner.
If you can just stay in the present,
that will help others a lot.

292

Forget about
how someone has offended you.
A small offense can destroy a great friendship,
don't let it.

293

Life has little meaning
for one without a home.
One who has a roof over their head
is pretty well off.

294

If you find something that you love to do,
you will never work another day in your life.

295

When one is helping another,
both gain in strength.

296

A ship in the harbor is safe,
but that's not what ships are for.

297

When we walk long enough
everyone changes places.
The most powerful lose sometimes.

298

The most spiritual word is: "reciprocity".

299

The most unspiritual word is: "exclusive".
When someone is exclusive,
they shut people out
of their mind and heart.

300

The three most spiritual words are:
"humility, humility, and humility."
No matter what your position,
you need to be humble.

301

Forgive every person from your heart
or ask God to forgive them.

302

Politeness is not sold in the bazaar.

303

Friendship is not a fruit for enjoyment only,
but it also can be
an opportunity for service.

304

Excel in generosity.
Most of what you have
is just borrowed for a while.

305

Happiness, where are you going to?
There, where friendship exists
and the people are kind.

306

Giving your child a skill,
is better than giving them
a thousand pieces of gold.

307

Life is a mixture of joy and sorrow.

308

Do a good deed,
then throw it into the sea,
or tell others about it
and they may be inspired to copy you
and do their own good deeds.

309

Wake up happy!
While you are waking up, practice smiling.
Smile every chance you get.

310

Take an oath to do no harm.
Harmlessness is the ultimate power.

311

It is best to bandage the finger
before it is cut.

312

Do good if you want to receive good.
What goes around, comes around.

313

Glory is found in the family.

314

People will not bend low enough
to hear what God says.

315

The donkey called the rooster:
"big-headed".

316

Some spiritual people
take an oath of poverty
to keep their lives simple.

317

Have the grace to laugh at yourself.

318

Having a good conversation
is like having riches.

319

No person is born great.
Great people become great
while others are sleeping.

320

Don't be afraid to be different.
Your uniqueness is what makes you special.

321

If it rained soup,
the poor would only have forks.

322

Don't be like a shadow,
a companion,
but not a comrade.

323

Misfortune teaches us to pray.

324

Just before a kind person stumbles
into a ditch in the darkness,
lightning will light up their path.

325

If someone slams you
with a negative comment,
you don't have to slam them back.
You can respond lovingly or silently.

326

The person who has no sibling,
is like a person at the front in battle.

327

Just because you can,
doesn't mean you should.

328

Good character
will never forsake its owner.

329

Until you can get a horse,
saddle a donkey.
Your own donkey
is better than someone else's horse.

330

Some people try to please God.

331

We have to be warriors
for our own survival.
We are in the awkward position
as the earth's shepherds.
This is the eleventh hour.

332

When one door shuts,
a thousand open.

333

Through collaboration and cooperation,
the most difficult challenges
can be overcome.

334

Don't be so in love
that you can't tell it's raining.

335

The love in your heart is worth more
than all the money in the world.

336

One of the best things you can give a child
is your undivided attention. Listen.

337

Run away from a tiger on the land,
to face a crocodile in the water.

338

Since life is short,
shouldn't we meet again?

339

Don't climb the pole of the marquis,
to show your alms giving.

340

To respect the holiness of the earth,
you could form the habit of going barefoot.

341

A person of words,
who is not a person of deeds,
is like a garden full of weeds.

342

If you dig a hole for someone else,
you may fall into it yourself.

343

A dog that always barks
gets little attention.

344

Life is short,
but it barely takes a second to smile.

345

A donkey with a load of holy books,
is still a donkey.

346

Love is like a baby,
it needs to be treated tenderly.

347

God will remain,
friends may not.

348

Love, like rain,
doesn't decide which grass it rains on.

349

In a deep relationship,
people always pick up
right where they left off.

350

Our greatest wealth is:
our children and our old people.
The babies and elders
help us to slow down.

351

A clear mind is more precious than gold.
When you are clear inside,
you are less likely
to cause anything problematic.

352

Friends for a meal are easy to find.
Friends until the end of life
are difficult to find.

353

A raven is the aunt of a blue jay.

354

A clever person is able to teach civility.

355

Indigenous people
have relationships in their relationships.
These fortunate people are utterly real.

356

The way to overcome an angry person
is with gentleness,
a mean person with sweetness,
a miser with generosity
and a liar with the truth,
but some people just have to be avoided.

357

Worldly people go outward,
but we must seek seclusion like a tortuga
who withdraws into its shell for an inner journey.

358

The wisdom of the elders
is the wealth of the village.

359

Don't throw away the old bucket,
until you know
whether the new one holds water.

360

A wise person has one house,
a rich person has two.

361

Love and arrogance don't go together.

362

All the people who live under one sky
are woven together like one big tapestry.

363

God has not forgotten anyone,
it is ignorance of God's timing,
which is what makes us complain.

364

The truly wise person is never selfish.

365

Don't sell the bearskin
until you have caught the bear.

366

If you lift together, it's better,
even if it's only a sheet of paper.

367

Judge yourself before someone else does.
Be so busy improving yourself,
that you have no time to criticize others.

368

A rich person gains from their generosity.

369

Wild bears keep each other company.

370

It takes a whole village to raise a child.

371

It is better to be blind,
than to see things
from only one point of view.
A narrow-minded person is troublesome.

372

Equality is a promise of a better life for all.

373

Don't want anyone who doesn't want you.
Let them go.
Perhaps your way of life
is too much for them.

374

Everything you do,
do it with love.

375

It is better to be loved than feared.

376

A false friend and a shadow
only show up when the sun is shining.

377

Because of bad things
that happen in the world,
some people are mad at God.
After they die,
maybe they will be able to
take God to court.
If God lived on earth,
some people
would break out all of God's windows.

378

To the swift horse, one flick of a switch,
to the intelligent person, one word.

379

The mind is not open for another to see.

380

A happy person keeps getting younger.

381

Never say: "I regret".
Always say: "I learned".

382

To the mediocre,
mediocrity seems great.

383

Love is like the wind, you can't see it,
but you can feel it.
If you need to be a priority,
but you are just an option,
retreat from the "love" that you cannot feel.

384

The determined ostrich hunter will surely find one.

385

A beautiful, communal, magic meadow
is ruined by the bears.

386

A person who plants trees
under whose shade they will never sit,
is a truly great person.

387

Love is blind and jealousy sees too much.

388

Money will buy a fine dog,
but only kindness can make it wag its tail.

389

Time lapses,
and an ungrateful person
forgets past kindnesses.

390

Sometimes it's better not to interfere
with another person's destiny.

391

After the pitch darkness,
most assuredly comes the dawn.

392

God hates lies.
People hate the truth,
yet, there is no third option.

393

You may have to teach mean people
to treat you kindly,
but you can't teach a crab to walk straight.

394

Don't surrender
to your first idea or thought,
slow down,
and think about all of the possibilities.

395

If you need to determine
who your real friends are,
mess up very badly,
your real friends will still be there.

396

A frog beneath a coconut shell
knows nothing of the great sea.

397

If you live with the wolves,
you will have to howl like a wolf.

398

With manners anything can be obtained.
Manners Maketh Humans

399

The egg thinks it's smarter than the hen.

400

One who is unselfish
can care for one who is selfish,
but the one who is selfish
will only care about themselves.

401

Everything you learn
is what you will take with you when you die.

402

A proverb is to speech,
what salt is to food.

403

The friends of our friends, are our friends.
The enemies of our enemies are our friends.

404

Understanding
is the bridge built by conversations.
Build bridges not walls.

405

A person who is not grateful,
complains about many things.
Work at gratitude.

406

The truly rich are
those who enjoy what they already have.

407

Pinning your hopes on God only,
you could get nothing.

408

Don't give and then take.
Don't love and then hate.

409

If the prayers of dogs were answered,
bones would rain from the sky.

410

Every person in your life is a teacher.
Some bring lessons about love and support,
others teach you what to avoid.

411

When a prayer is answered,
the person who prayed
becomes overwhelmed.

412

Punctuality is the politeness of monarchs.

413

If you are filled with pride,
then you will leave no room for wisdom.

414

Day breaks for a hen's cackle
and a rooster's crow.

415

The old dog barks while it is sitting down.

416

As small as it is,
a sparrow has all the right parts.

417

Good character is a person's adornment,
it is real beauty that never fades.

418

Desire for haste causes delays.
One who takes things slowly, goes far.

419

When you are warmhearted
your own soul is nourished.
Your own soul is damaged
when you are coldhearted.

420

An independent person
who values their own freedom,
may wander as solitary
as a rhinoceros horn.

421

Done by oneself, is well done.

422

"Revenge is mine": sayeth God,
"I will repay".
Never take revenge.

423

The poor search for food
and the rich search for hunger.

424

When you are open to receiving them,
the opportunities keep coming.

425

Every act of creation is an act of love.

426

Slander cannot destroy a good person.
When the flood recedes the rock is still there.
One who knows their honor
must not be upset by slander.

427

Consider all delays as more time gained.
Patience is the key to everything.

428

At the feast of ego,
everyone leaves hungry.

429

Love someone when they least deserve it,
because that's when
they need love the most.

430

In choosing a friend,
go up a step.

431

A person may say they love you.
Wait and see what they do for you.
Love has to be shown by deeds,
not by words.
A person who loves you,
will sacrifice for you.

432

Two tigers cannot share one mountain.

433

Little by little, the bird makes its nest.
Everything is a process that takes time.

434

The earth is a small place for fugitives.

435

A crowded room is better than an empty castle.

436

Communicate your love wholeheartedly.

437

It's too late to close the stable door,
after the horse has bolted.

438

It's better to retreat in honor,
than to advance in disgrace.

439

Fifty million flies
can be wrong in a greasy-spoon-diner.
Just because a lot of people like something,
that doesn't mean it's right for you.

440

Although some plans may never bear fruit,
People should still make plans.

441

It takes two to make a quarrel,
but only one to end it.
It is the wise person who quits.

442

Lies that build
are better than truths that destroy.

443

Old people deserve respect and a medal.

444

Kindness can be a religion.

445

A rising tide raises all the boats.

446

It is easy to dislike what you cannot get.

447

If you know how to take,
learn how to give.
True happiness is when
you can start giving back.

448

When you buy things you don't need,
you are stealing from yourself.

449

The old horse in the stable,
still yearns to gallop back to the stable.

450

Don't praise what is yours,
and belittle what is another's.

451

God lets things go, but only up to a point.
God provides, but just in the nick of time.

452

It's much better to be alone
than in bad company;
not my circus, not my monkeys.

453

Beauty is an empty calabash.

454

The goat's business is not the pig's affair.

455

A flea can trouble a lion
more than a lion can trouble a flea.

456

It is better to have a thousand enemies outside the tent,
than one inside the tent.

457

There is a bit of the jerk in everyone,
try to keep that to a minimum.

458

Traveling gives you a home
in a thousand strange places,
then leaves you a stranger
in your own land.

459

A fish and a bird may fall in love
and have an interesting time building together.

460

If you do something wrong,
say: "I'm sorry".
When someone apologizes,
say: "I forgive you".

461

Sometimes, a little bit of something
is better than nothing.

462

Who doesn't know the falcon will cook it.

463

A thief believes that everybody steals.
What you see in yourself,
is what you see in the world.

464

Walk a mile in my moccasins
to find out where they pinch.

465

Character is often corrupted by prosperity.

466

The mills of God grind slowly,
but they grind exceedingly fine.

467

Don't saw off the branch
that you are sitting on.

468

Love will find a way,
indifference will find an excuse.

469

You learn how to cut trees down,
by cutting down trees.

470

Emotions are like wild horses,
they are sometimes difficult to control.

471

Short prayers reach Heaven.

472

If you keep advising a heedless person,
you yourself are in need of advice.

473

Be transparent to the world,
and let the world be transparent to you.
Allow your soul to shine through you.

474

The early bird catches the worm,
but the night owl finds the best parties.

475

Deep calleth unto deep.

476

Salt does not boast that it is salty.

477

No response can be a powerful one.
Sometimes silence has a mighty noise.

478

Speak about the good qualities
of your dead people.

479

Forcing people to do what they do not
want to do,
is like trying to fill the ocean with rocks.

480

Respect yourself,
and others
will be more likely to respect you.

481

The sky is wide enough
for all the birds to fly without colliding.

482

Live in thankfulness for the richness
which makes life so precious.

483

It is for the benefit of the blind
that thunder rumbles.
It is for the benefit of deaf people
that lightning flashes.

484

A person without culture
is like a zebra without stripes.

485

If it ain't broke, don't fix it.

486

Experience nature to learn about yourself.

487

As you teach, you learn
and one who learns, teaches.

488

Mutual affection gives each their share.

489

Try to leave
every person, place, or condition,
better than when you first got there.

490

Hunger is good sauce.
Hunger makes any food taste good.

491

All the contests are over.
Everybody won!

492

Once you have something,
don't take it for granted.
What's at home, counts.

493

A good friend is like a four leaf clover.
Anyone with a good friend is lucky,
because good friends are rare.

494

Random acts of kindness
make everyone feel better.

495

One who waits to see a crab wink,
will tarry long upon the shore.

496

Unless a person is simple,
they cannot recognize God.

497

The early bird gets the worm,
but the late mouse gets the cheese.

498

Seek wisdom like a beggar.
Wisdom can protect us.
A drop of wisdom
is better than a sea of gold.

499

The world goes forth, and we follow.

500

Almost everything has an end,
except for the banana which has two.

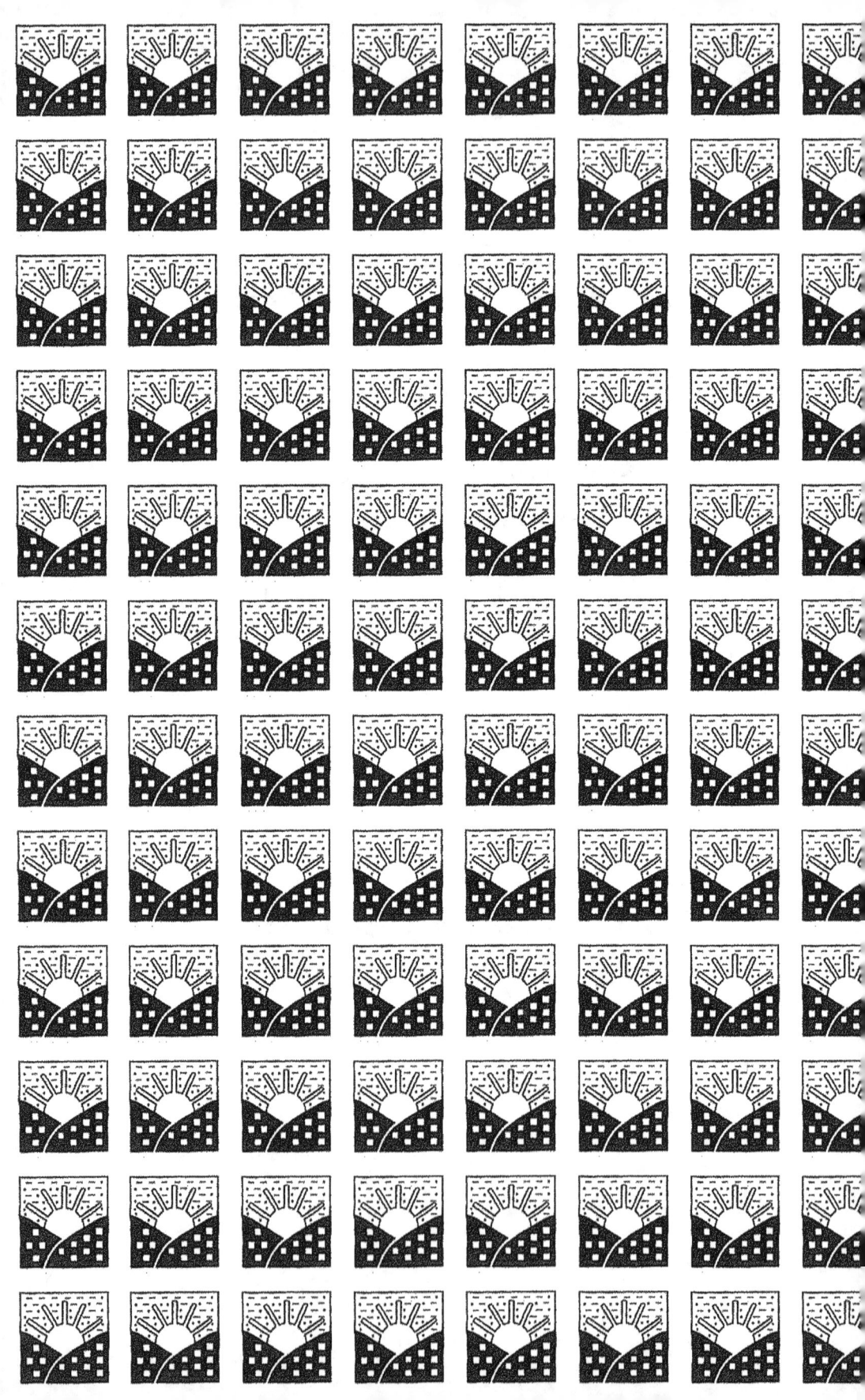

www.ingramcontent.com/pod-product-compliance
Lightning Source LLC
LaVergne TN
LVHW022000060526
838201LV00048B/1634